Peter Ilyich

TCHAIKOVSKY

OVERTURE 1812

Op. 49

Edited by

Richard W. Sargeant, Jr.

Study Score
Partitur

SERENISSIMA MUSIC, INC.

ORCHESTRA

Piccolo
2 Flutes
2 Oboes
English Horn
2 Clarinets (B-flat)
2 Bassoons

4 Horns (F)
2 Trumpets (C)*
2 Cornets (B-flat)
3 Trombones
Tuba

Timpani
Percussion
Snare Drum, Bass Drum, Cymbals, Tambourine,
Triangle, Chimes, Cannon
Brass Band
4 Horns, 2 Cornets, 2 Trombones, Basses,
Snare Drum, Bass Drum, Cymbals, Chimes

Violin I
Violin II
Viola
Violoncello
Double Bass

*The present score has been updated for the common keys of modern instruments
(Clarinets in A or B-flat, Horns in F, Trumpets in C). The original score featured
Trumpets in E-flat.

Duration: ca. 16 minutes

Premiere: August 20, 1882
Moscow, Russia
Art and Industry Exposition
Orchestra / Ippolit Altani

ISBN: 978-1-60874-219-6
This score is a newly-engraved edition prepared from the composer's manuscript
and the first edition of the score and parts.
Printed in the USA
First Printing: August, 2018

OVERTURE 1812
Op. 49

Pyotr Tchaikovsky
Edited by Richard W. Sargeant, Jr.

4

26
34
Picc.
Fl.
Ob.
E. H.
Cl.
Bn.
Hn.
Tpt.
Cor.
Trb.
Tuba
Timp.
S. D.
Cymb. B. D
Perc.
Br. Band
Vn.
Va.
Vc.
Cb.
più f
cresc.
f
ff
f cresc.
p
tutti
tutti unis.

36
Picc.
Fl. 1 2
a2
Ob. 1 2
1.
f piangendo (lamentingly) e molto espress.
E. H.
Cl. 1 2
a2
Bn. 1 2
Hn. 1 2
3 4
Tpt. 1 2
1.
Cor. 1 2
Trb. 1 2
3 Tuba
Timp.
S. D.
Cymb. B. D
Perc.
Br. Band
36
Vn. 1 2
sfp
Va.
unis.
Vc.
unis.
mf
sf
Cb.

45
Picc.
Fl. 1 2
Ob. 1 2
E. H.
Cl. 1 2
Bn. 1 2
a2
1.
mf
f
Hn. 1 2 3 4
Tpt. 1 2
Cor. 1 2
Trb. 1 2 3
Tuba
Timp.
S. D.
Cymb. B. D
Perc.
Br. Band
45
Vn. 1 2
Va.
Vc.
Cb.
pizz.

52
poco string.
Picc.
Fl. 1 2
Ob. 1 2
E. H.
Cl. 1 2
Bn. 1 2
Hn. 1 2 3 4
Tpt. 1 2
Cor. 1 2
Trb. 1 2 3
Tuba
Timp.
S. D.
Cymb. B. D
Perc.
Br. Band
Vn. 1 2
Va.
Vc.
Cb.
mf
f
cresc.
arco

57
58 poco più mosso
Picc.
Fl. 1 2
a2
Ob. 1 2
E. H.
Cl. 1 2
Bn. 1 2
marcatissimo
Hn. 1 2 3 4
Tpt. 1 2
Cor. 1 2
Trb. 1 2 3
Tuba
Timp.
S. D.
Cymb. B. D
Perc.
Br. Band
57
58 poco più mosso
Vn. 1 2
Va.
Vc.
Cb.
ff
fff
marcatissimo

62
Picc.
Fl. 1 2
Ob. 1 2
E. H.
Cl. 1 2
Bn. 1 2
a2
Hn. 1 2 3 4
fff
Tpt. 1 2
Cor. 1 2
Trb. 1 2 3
Tuba
Timp.
S. D.
Cymb. B. D
ff
Perc.
Br. Band
Vn. 1 2
Va.
Vc.
Cb.

68
Picc.
Fl. 1 2
Ob. 1 2
E. H.
Cl. 1 2
Bn. 1 2
Hn. 1 2 3 4
Tpt. 1 2
Cor. 1 2
Trb. 1 2 3
Tuba
Timp.
S. D.
Cymb. B. D
Perc.
Br. Band
Vn. 1 2
Va.
Vc.
Cb.
fff

77 Andante ♩= 80
Picc.
Fl. 1 2
Ob. 1 2
E. H.
Cl. 1 2
Bn. 1 2
Hn. 1 2
Hn. 3 4
Tpt. 1 2
Cor. 1 2
Trb. 1 2
3 Tuba
Timp.
S. D.
Cymb. B. D
Perc.
Br. Band
77 Andante ♩= 80
Vn. 1
Vn. 2
Va.
Vc.
Cb.
mf
p
sf

82
Picc.
Fl. 1 2
Ob. 1 2
E. H.
Cl. 1 2
Bn. 1 2
Hn. 1 2
3 4
Tpt. 1 2
Cor. 1 2
Trb. 1 2
3
Tuba
Timp.
S. D.
Cymb. B. D
Perc.
Br. Band
82
Vn. 1
2
Va.
Vc.
Cb.
mf

87
Picc.
Fl. 1 2
Ob. 1 2
E. H.
Cl. 1 2
Bn. 1 2
Hn. 1 2
3 4
Tpt. 1 2
Cor. 1 2
Trb. 1 2
3 Tuba
Timp.
S. D.
Cymb. B. D
Perc.
Br. Band
87
Vn. 1
2
Va.
Vc.
Cb.
sf
p
1.
pp
mf

92
96
Allegro giusto ♩ = 138
Picc.
Fl. 1 2
Ob. 1 2
E. H.
Cl. 1 2
Bn. 1 2
Hn. 1 2
3 4
Tpt. 1 2
Cor. 1 2
Trb. 1 2
3 Tuba
Timp.
S. D.
Cymb. B. D
Perc.
Br. Band
Vn. 1
2
Va.
Vc.
Cb.
f
pp
mf
p

99
Picc.
Fl. 1 2
Ob. 1 2
E. H.
Cl. 1 2
Bn. 1 2
1.
Hn. 1 2
3 4
Tpt. 1 2
Cor. 1 2
Trb. 1 2
3 Tuba
Timp.
S. D.
Cymb. B. D
Perc.
Br. Band
99
Vn. 1
2
Va.
Vc.
Cb.
ff

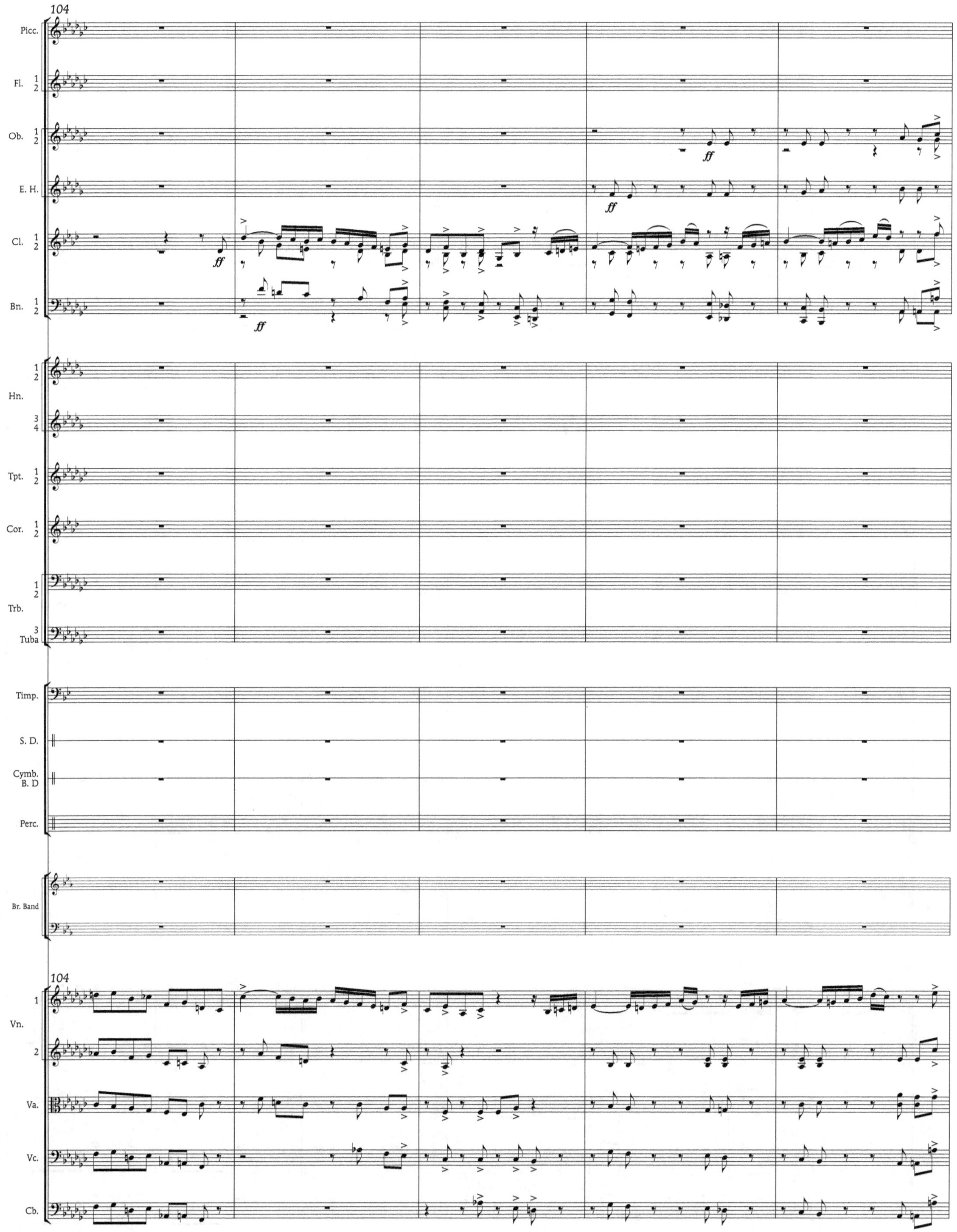
104
Picc.
Fl. 1 2
Ob. 1 2
E. H.
Cl. 1 2
Bn. 1 2
ff
Hn. 1 2 3 4
Tpt. 1 2
Cor. 1 2
Trb. 1 2 3
Tuba
Timp.
S. D.
Cymb. B. D
Perc.
Br. Band
104
Vn. 1 2
Va.
Vc.
Cb.

109
Picc.
ff
a2
Fl. 1 2
ff
Ob. 1 2
E. H.
Cl. 1 2
Bn. 1 2
Hn. 1 2
ff
3 4
ff
Tpt. 1 2
Cor. 1 2
Trb. 1 2
1.
f
cresc.
3 Tuba
f
Timp.
S. D.
Cymb. B. D
Perc.
Br. Band
109
Vn. 1
2
div.
Va.
Vc.
Cb.

117
115
Picc.
Fl. 1 2
a2
Ob. 1 2
E. H.
Cl. 1 2
a2
Bn. 1 2
Hn. 1 2
3 4
Tpt. 1 2
ff
Cor. 1 2
1.
ff
Trb. 1 2
ff
3
Tuba
cresc.
ff
Timp.
ff
S. D.
Cymb. B. D
ff
Perc.
Br. Band
117
115
Vn. 1
2
unis.
Va.
Vc.
Cb.

20

42196

123
Picc.
Fl. 1 2
a2
Ob. 1 2
f
E. H.
Cl. 1 2
Bn. 1 2
Hn. 1 2
3 4
Tpt. 1 2
Cor. 1 2
a2
f marc.
Trb. 1 2
3 Tuba
Timp.
S. D.
pp
Cymb. B. D
Perc.
Br. Band
123
Vn. 1
2
Va.
Vc.
Cb.

126
Picc.
Fl. 1 2
Ob. 1 2
1.
E. H.
f
Cl. 1 2
Bn. 1 2
Hn. 1 2
f marc.
3 4
f marc.
Tpt. 1 2
Cor. 1 2
Trb. 1 2
3
Tuba
Timp.
S. D.
f
pp
Cymb. B. D
Perc.
Br. Band
126
Vn. 1
2
Va.
Vc.
Cb.

130
Picc.
Fl. 1 2
a2
Ob. 1 2
a2
E. H.
Cl. 1 2
a2
Bn. 1 2
a2
Hn. 1 2
3 4
Tpt. 1 2
a2
f marc.
Cor. 1 2
Trb. 1 2
3
Tuba
Timp.
S. D.
p
Cymb. B. D
Perc.
Br. Band
130
Vn. 1
2
Va.
Vc.
Cb.

134
Picc.
Fl. 1 2
Ob. 1 2
E. H.
Cl. 1 2
Bn. 1 2
Hn. 1 2 3 4
Tpt. 1 2
Cor. 1 2
Trb. 1 2 3
Tuba
Timp.
S. D.
Cymb. B. D
Perc.
Br. Band
134
Vn. 1 2
Va.
Vc.
Cb.
cresc.
ff
f
p
1.

139
143
Picc.
Fl. 1 2
a2
fff
Ob. 1 2
E. H.
Cl. 1 2
Bn. 1 2
Hn. 1 2 3 4
Tpt. 1 2
1.
Cor. 1 2
Trb. 1 2 3
Tuba
Timp.
S. D.
Cymb. B. D
Perc.
Br. Band
Vn. 1 2
Va.
Vc.
Cb.

144
Picc.
fff
Fl. 1 2
Ob. 1 2
E. H.
Cl. 1 2
Bn. 1 2
Hn. 1 2 3 4
Tpt. 1 2
Cor. 1 2
Trb. 1 2 3
Tuba
Timp.
S. D.
Cymb. B. D
ff
Perc.
Br. Band
144
Vn. 1 2
Va.
Vc.
Cb.

149
Picc.
Fl. 1 2
a2
Ob. 1 2
a2
E. H.
Cl. 1 2
a2
Bn. 1 2
a2
Hn. 1 2
3 4
Tpt. 1 2
Cor. 1 2
Trb. 1 2
3 Tuba
Timp.
S. D.
Cymb. B. D
fff
Perc.
Br. Band
149
Vn. 1
2
Va.
Vc.
Cb.

156
Picc.
Fl. 1 2
Ob. 1 2
fff
E. H.
Cl. 1 2
fff
Bn. 1 2
fff
Hn. 1 2
ff
ff
3 4
ff
ff
Tpt. 1 2
Cor. 1 2
Trb. 1 2
3 Tuba
Timp.
S. D.
Cymb. B. D
Perc.
Br. Band
156
Vn. 1
2
Va.
Vc.
Cb.

163 L'istesso tempo
Picc.
Fl.
Ob.
E. H.
Cl.
Bn.
Hn.
Tpt.
Cor.
Trb.
Tuba
Timp.
S. D.
Cymb.
B. D
Perc.
Tgl.
Br. Band
163 L'istesso tempo
Vn.
Va.
Vc.
Cb.
p cresc.

174
Picc.
Fl. 1 2
Ob. 1 2
E. H.
Cl. 1 2
Bn. 1 2
Hn. 1 2 3 4
Tpt. 1 2
Cor. 1 2
Trb. 1 2 3
Tuba
Timp.
S. D.
Cymb. B. D
Perc.
Br. Band
174
Vn. 1 2
Va.
Vc.
Cb.
f sempre
f

184
187
Picc.
Fl. 1 2
ff
f sempre
Ob. 1 2
a2
E. H.
Cl. 1 2
Bn. 1 2
Hn. 1 2
Hn. 3 4
Tpt. 1 2
Cor. 1 2
Trb. 1 2
Trb. 3 Tuba
Timp.
S. D.
Cymb. B. D
Perc.
Br. Band
Vn. 1
Vn. 2
Va.
Vc.
Cb.
3

193
Picc.
Fl. 1 2
Ob. 1 2
E. H.
Cl. 1 2
Bn. 1 2
Hn. 1 2
3 4
Tpt. 1 2
Cor. 1 2
Trb. 1 2
3
Tuba
Timp.
S. D.
Cymb. B. D
Perc.
Br. Band
193
Vn. 1
2
Va.
Vc.
Cb.

202
207 L'istesso tempo
Picc.
Fl. 1 2
Ob. 1 2
E. H.
Cl. 1 2
Bn. 1 2
Hn. 1 2 3 4
Tpt. 1 2
Cor. 1 2
Trb. 1 2 3
Tuba
Timp.
S. D.
Cymb. B. D
Perc.
Tamb.
Br. Band
Vn. 1 2
Va.
Vc.
Cb.
mf
p
ppp
pp sempre
1.
2.

34

42196

217
Picc.
Fl. 1 2
Ob. 1 2
E. H.
Cl. 1 2
1.
Bn. 1 2
1.
p
Hn. 1 2
3 4
Tpt. 1 2
Cor. 1 2
Trb. 1 2
3 Tuba
Timp.
S. D.
Cymb. B. D
Perc.
Br. Band
217
Vn. 1
2
Va.
Vc.
pp
Cb.

224
Picc.
Fl. 1 2
Ob. 1 2
E. H.
Cl. 1 2
Bn. 1 2
1.
mf
Hn. 1 2 3 4
a2
mf marc.
cresc.
Tpt. 1 2
1.
mf
Cor. 1 2
Trb. 1 2
1.
mf
3 Tuba
Timp.
S. D.
ppp
mp
ppp
Cymb. B. D
Perc.
Br. Band
224
Vn. 1 2
pp
mf cresc.
più f
f
Va.
pp
mf cresc.
più f
f
Vc.
mf cresc.
più f
f
Cb.
pp
mf cresc.
più f
f

231
Picc.
Fl. 1 2
Ob. 1 2
1.
mf
E. H.
Cl. 1 2
f
sf
Bn. 1 2
Hn. 1 2 3 4
a2
mf marc.
Tpt. 1 2
Cor. 1 2
Trb. 1 2 3
Tuba
Timp.
S. D.
ppp
mp
Cymb. B. D
Perc.
Br. Band
231
Vn. 1 2
Va.
Vc.
Cb.
mf cresc.
più f

237
Picc.
Fl. 1 2
Ob. 1 2
mf
E. H.
Cl. 1 2
f
sf
Bn. 1 2
1.
mf
f
sf
Hn. 1 2
f
sf
3 4
cresc.
f
sf
Tpt. 1 2
Cor. 1 2
mf
Trb. 1 2
mf
3 Tuba
Timp.
S. D.
ppp
Cymb. B. D
Perc.
Br. Band
237
Vn. 1
f
cresc.
2
f
cresc.
Va.
f
cresc.
Vc.
f
cresc.
Cb.
f
cresc.

243
244
Picc.
Fl. 1 2
a2
ff
Ob. 1 2
E. H.
Cl. 1 2
Bn. 1 2
Hn. 1 2
Hn. 3 4
Tpt. 1 2
Cor. 1 2
Trb. 1 2
Trb. 3 Tuba
Timp.
S. D.
Cymb. B. D
Perc.
Br. Band
243
244
Vn. 1
Vn. 2
Va.
Vc.
Cb.

247
Picc.
Fl. 1 2
Ob. 1 2
E. H.
Cl. 1 2
Bn. 1 2
Hn. 1 2
3 4
Tpt. 1 2
Cor. 1 2
Trb. 1 2
3 Tuba
Timp.
S. D.
Cymb. B. D
Perc.
Br. Band
247
Vn. 1
2
Va.
Vc.
Cb.

251
Picc.
Fl. 1 2
Ob. 1 2
E. H.
Cl. 1 2
Bn. 1 2
Hn. 1 2 3 4
Tpt. 1 2
Cor. 1 2
Trb. 1 2 3
Tuba
Timp.
S. D.
Cymb. B. D
Perc.
Br. Band
251
Vn. 1 2
div.
Va.
Vc.
Cb.

256
258
Picc.
Fl. 1 2
a2
fff
Ob. 1 2
E. H.
Cl. 1 2
Bn. 1 2
Hn. 1 2 3 4
Tpt. 1 2
Cor. 1 2
Trb. 1 2 3
Tuba
Timp.
S. D.
Cymb. B. D
Perc.
Br. Band
Vn. 1 2
Va.
unis.
Vc.
Cb.

260
Picc.
fff
Fl. 1 2
Ob. 1 2
E. H.
Cl. 1 2
Bn. 1 2
Hn. 1 2
3 4
Tpt. 1 2
Cor. 1 2
Trb. 1 2
3 Tuba
Timp.
S. D.
Cymb. B. D
fff
Perc.
Br. Band
260
Vn. 1
2
Va.
Vc.
Cb.

265
Picc.
Fl. 1 2
a2
Ob. 1 2
1.
E. H.
Cl. 1 2
a2
Bn. 1 2
a2
Hn. 1 2
ff
Hn. 3 4
ff
Tpt. 1 2
Cor. 1 2
Trb. 1 2
Trb. 3
Tuba
f
Timp.
S. D.
Cymb. B. D
Perc.
Br. Band
265
Vn. 1
Vn. 2
Va.
Vc.
Cb.
fff

271
Picc.
Fl. 1 2
Ob. 1 2
fff
E. H.
Cl. 1 2
fff
Bn. 1 2
fff
Hn. 1 2
ff
3 4
ff
Tpt. 1 2
Cor. 1 2
Trb. 1 2
3
Tuba
f
Timp.
S. D.
Cymb. B. D
Perc.
Br. Band
271
Vn. 1
2
Va.
Vc.
Cb.

277
279
Picc.
Fl. 1 2
Ob. 1 2
E. H.
Cl. 1 2
Bn. 1 2
Hn. 1 2
Hn. 3 4
Tpt. 1 2
Cor. 1 2
Trb. 1 2
Trb. 3 Tuba
Tuba
Timp.
S. D.
Cymb. B. D
Tgl.
Perc.
Br. Band
279
277
Vn. 1
Vn. 2
Va.
Vc.
Cb.
cresc.

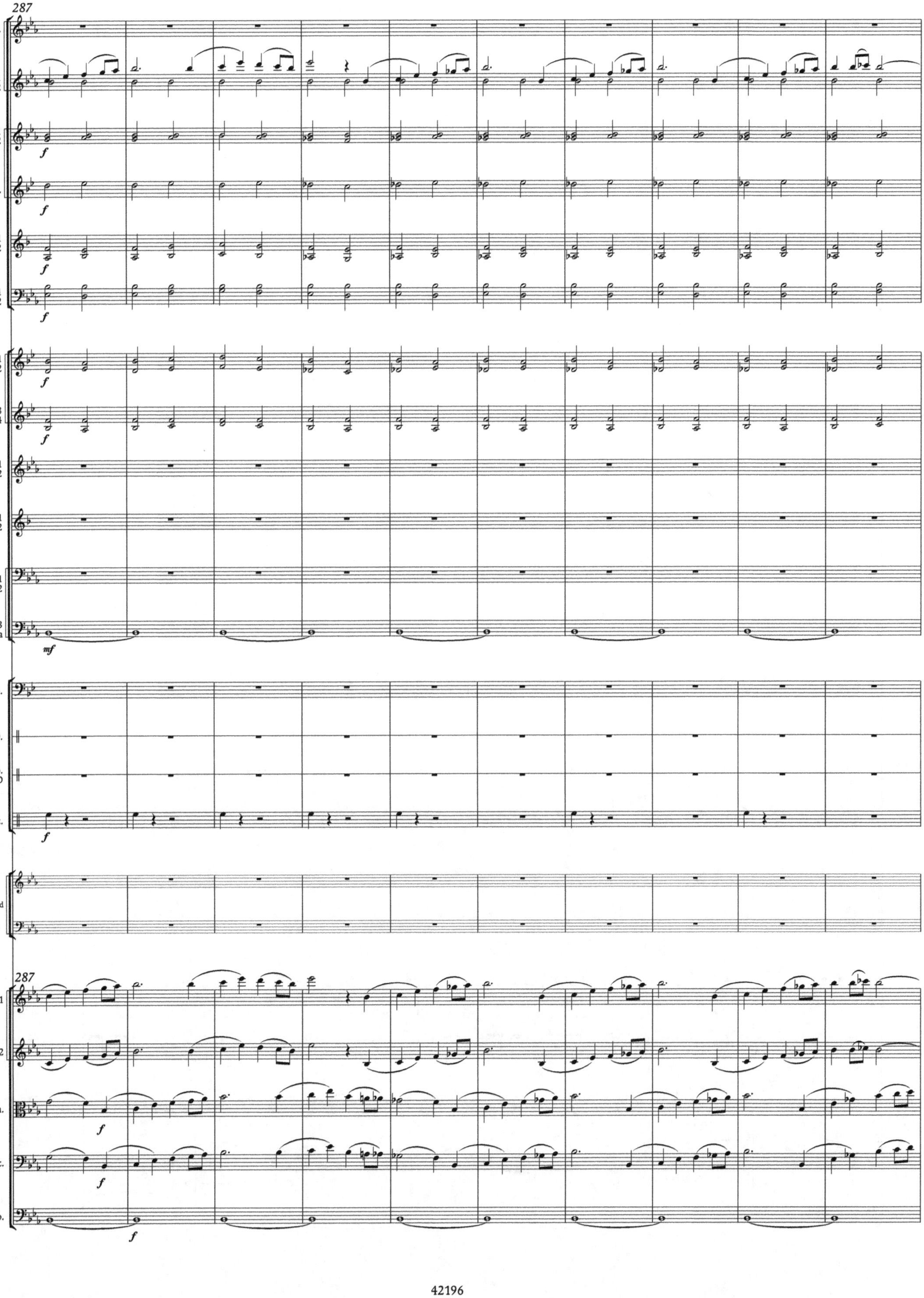
287
Picc.
Fl. 1 2
Ob. 1 2
E. H.
Cl. 1 2
Bn. 1 2
Hn. 1 2
Hn. 3 4
Tpt. 1 2
Cor. 1 2
Trb. 1 2
Trb. 3 Tuba
Timp.
S. D.
Cymb. B. D
Perc.
Br. Band
287
Vn. 1
Vn. 2
Va.
Vc.
Cb.
f
mf

48

42196

305
Picc.
Fl. 1 2
Ob. 1 2
E. H.
Cl. 1 2
Bn. 1 2
Hn. 1 2
mf
3.
Hn. 3 4
mf
Tpt. 1 2
Cor. 1 2
Trb. 1 2
3
Tuba
Timp.
pp
S. D.
Cymb. B. D
Perc.
Br. Band
305
Vn. 1
p
Vn. 2
p
Va.
p
Vc.
pizz.
arco
Cb.
pp

313
Picc.
Fl. 1 2
Ob. 1 2
E. H.
Cl. 1 2
Bn. 1 2
Hn. 1 2
Hn. 3 4
Tpt. 1 2
Cor. 1 2
Trb. 1 2
Trb. 3
Tuba
Timp.
S. D.
Cymb. B. D
Perc.
Br. Band
313
Vn. 1
Vn. 2
Va.
Vc.
Cb.
pp cresc. poco a poco
cresc. poco a poco
cresc. poco a poco

318
Picc.
Fl. 1 2
cresc. poco a poco
Ob. 1 2
cresc. poco a poco
E. H.
cresc. poco a poco
Cl. 1 2
cresc. poco a poco
Bn. 1 2
cresc. poco a poco
Hn. 1 2
cresc. poco a poco
3 4
cresc. poco a poco
Tpt. 1 2
Cor. 1 2
più f
Trb. 1 2
2.
mp cresc. poco a poco
3 Tuba
3.
mp cresc. poco a poco
Timp.
cresc. poco a poco
S. D.
cresc. poco a poco
Cymb. B. D
Perc.
Br. Band
318
Vn. 1
cresc. poco a poco
2
Va.
mp cresc. poco a poco
Vc.
Cb.

322
Picc.
Fl. 1 2
Ob. 1 2
E. H.
Cl. 1 2
Bn. 1 2
Hn. 1 2
3 4
Tpt. 1 2
Cor. 1 2
Trb. 1 2
3 Tuba
Timp.
S. D.
Cymb. B. D
Perc.
Br. Band
322
Vn. 1
2
Va.
Vc.
Cb.
mf cresc.
mf cresc. poco a poco

328
327
Picc.
Fl. 1 2
Ob. 1 2
E. H.
Cl. 1 2
Bn. 1 2
ff
a2
Hn. 1 2 3 4
Tpt. 1 2
marcatissimo
Cor. 1 2
Trb. 1 2 3
Tuba
Timp.
S. D.
Cymb. B. D
Tgl.
Perc.
Canon
Br. Band
Vn. 1 2
Va.
Vc.
Cb.

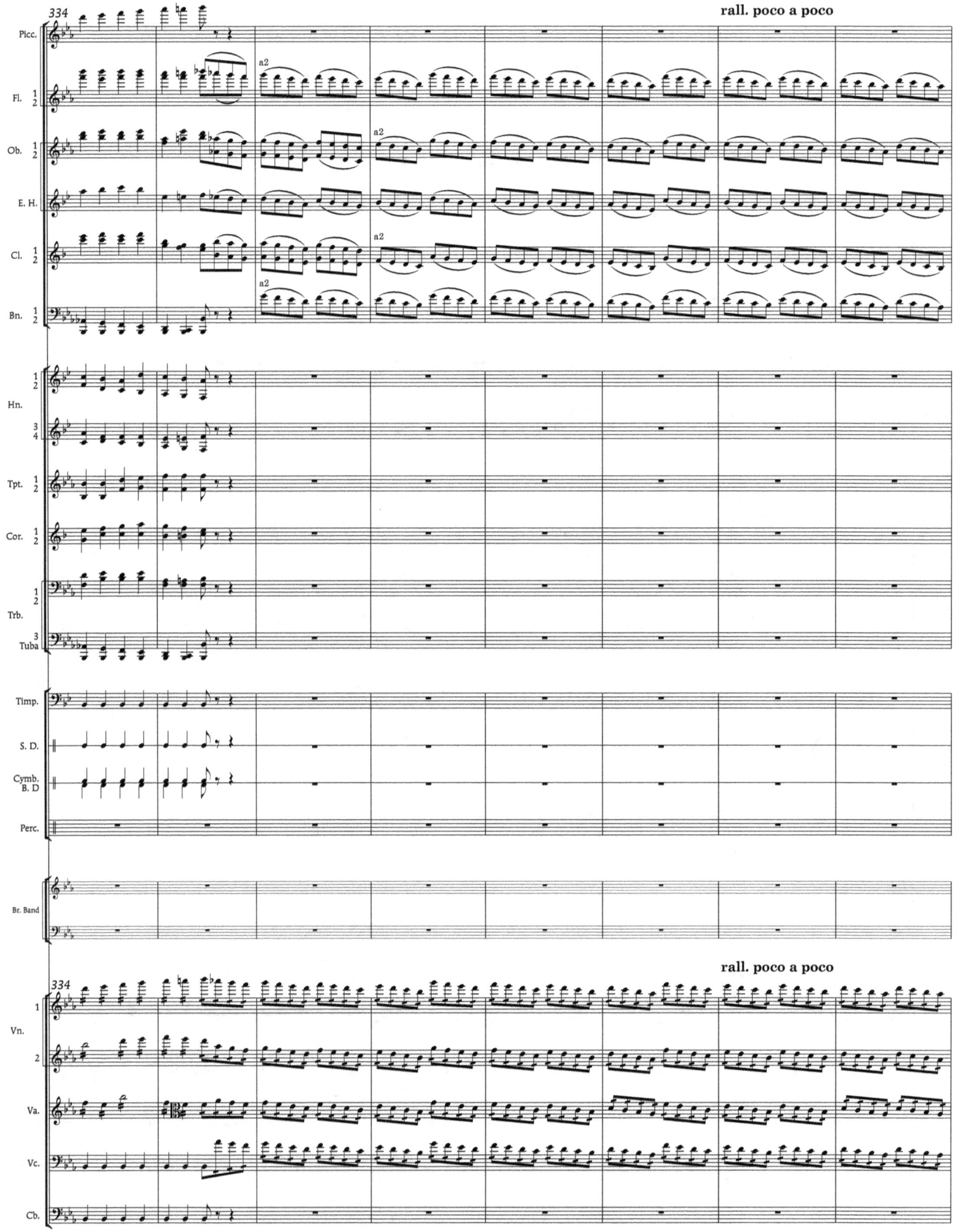
334
rall. poco a poco
Picc.
Fl. 1 2
a2
Ob. 1 2
E. H.
Cl. 1 2
Bn. 1 2
Hn. 1 2 3 4
Tpt. 1 2
Cor. 1 2
Trb. 1 2 3
Tuba
Timp.
S. D.
Cymb. B. D
Perc.
Br. Band
334
rall. poco a poco
Vn. 1 2
Va.
Vc.
Cb.

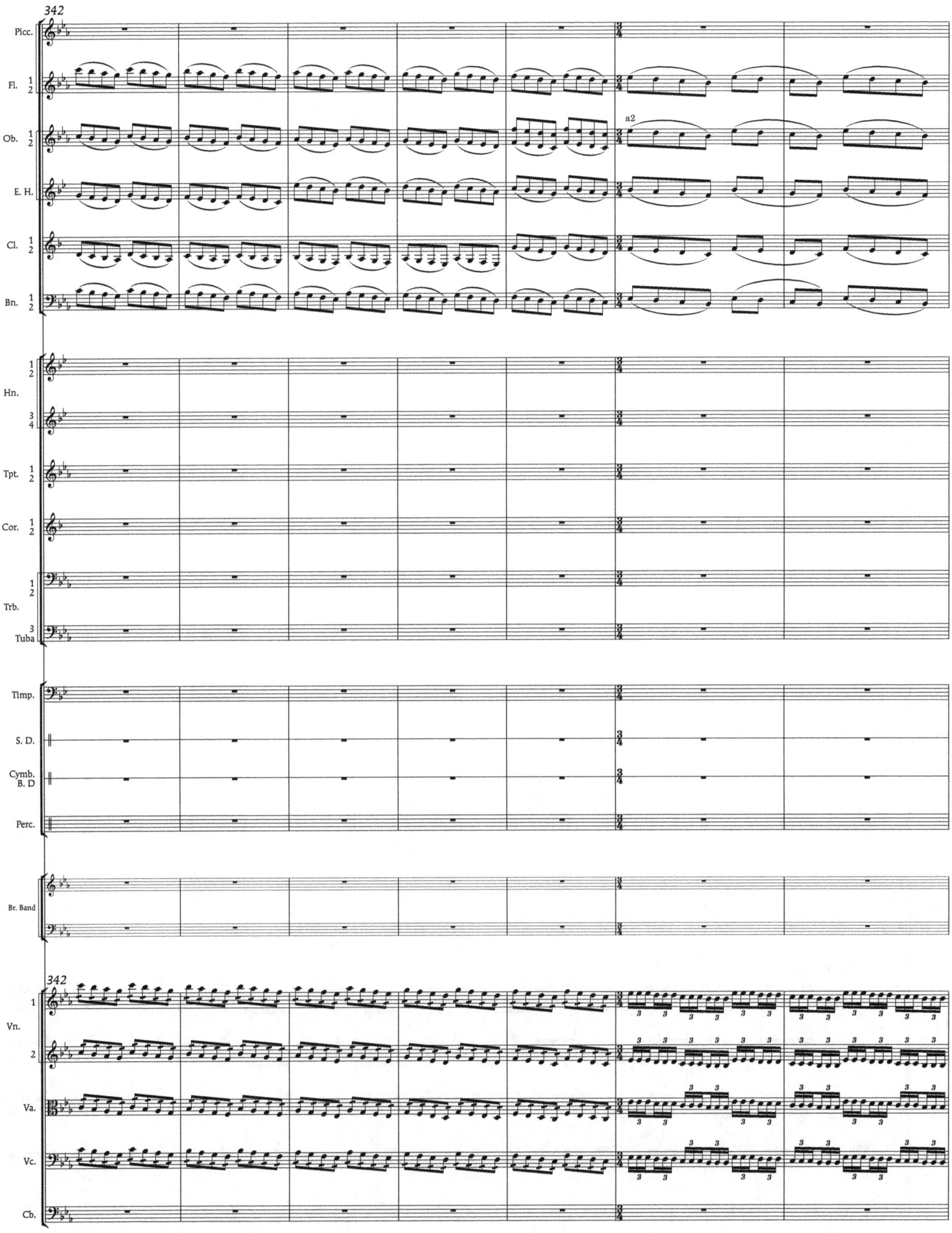
342
Picc.
Fl. 1 2
Ob. 1 2
a2
E. H.
Cl. 1 2
Bn. 1 2
Hn. 1 2 3 4
Tpt. 1 2
Cor. 1 2
Trb. 1 2 3
Tuba
Timp.
S. D.
Cymb. B. D
Perc.
Br. Band
342
Vn. 1 2
Va.
Vc.
Cb.

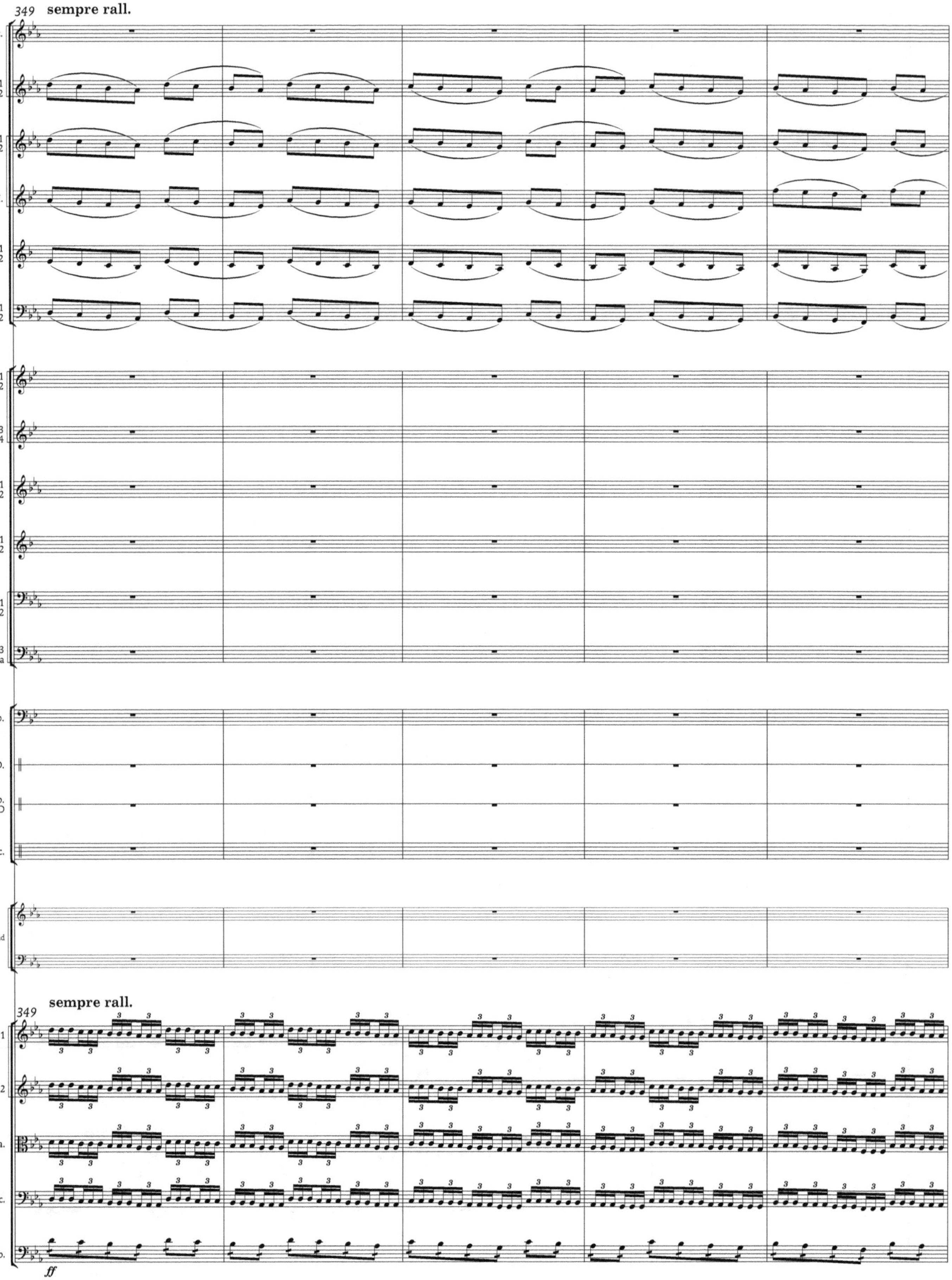
349
sempre rall.
Picc.
Fl. 1 2
Ob. 1 2
E. H.
Cl. 1 2
Bn. 1 2
Hn. 1 2
3 4
Tpt. 1 2
Cor. 1 2
Trb. 1 2
3
Tuba
Timp.
S. D.
Cymb. B. D
Perc.
Br. Band
349
sempre rall.
Vn. 1
2
Va.
Vc.
Cb.
ff

354
358
Largo ♩ = 60
Picc.
Fl.
Ob.
E. H.
Cl.
Bn.
Hn.
Tpt.
Cor.
Trb.
Tuba
Timp.
S. D.
Cymb. B. D
Perc.
Chimes
Br. Band
Vn.
Va.
Vc.
Cb.
cresc.
fff
f cresc.
ff cresc.
ff

361
Picc.
Fl. 1 2
Ob. 1 2
E. H.
Cl. 1 2
Bn. 1 2
Hn. 1 2
Hn. 3 4
Tpt. 1 2
Cor. 1 2
Trb. 1 2
3 Tuba
Timp.
S. D.
Cymb. B. D
Perc.
Br. Band
Vn. 1 2
Va.
Vc.
Cb.
fff
a2

368
Picc.
Fl. 1 2
a2
Ob. 1 2
E. H.
Cl. 1 2
Bn. 1 2
a2
fff
Hn. 1 2 3 4
Tpt. 1 2
Cor. 1 2
Trb. 1 2 3
Tuba
Timp.
S. D.
Cymb. B. D
Perc.
Br. Band
368
Vn. 1 2
Va.
Vc.
Cb.
fff

380 Allegro vivace
376
Picc.
Fl. 1 2
Ob. 1 2
E. H.
Cl. 1 2
Bn. 1 2
Hn. 1 2 3 4
Tpt. 1 2
Cor. 1 2
Trb. 1 2 3
Tuba
Timp.
S. D.
Cymb. B. D
Perc.
Br. Band
Vn. 1 2
Va.
div.
Vc.
Cb.
a2
fff
ff

383
Picc.
Fl. 1 2
Ob. 1 2
E. H.
Cl. 1 2
Bn. 1 2
Hn. 1 2
3 4
Tpt. 1 2
ffff
Cor. 1 2
a2
Trb. 1 2
ffff
a2
3 Tuba
Timp.
S. D.
Cymb. B. D
Canon
ffff
Perc.
Br. Band
383
Vn. 1
2
Va.
Vc.
Cb.

391
Picc.
Fl. 1 2
Ob. 1 2
E. H.
Cl. 1 2
Bn. 1 2
Hn. 1 2 3 4
Tpt. 1 2
Cor. 1 2
Trb. 1 2 3
Tuba
Timp.
S. D.
Cymb. B. D
Perc.
Br. Band
391
Vn. 1 2
unis.
Va.
Vc.
Cb.

399
Picc.
Fl. 1 2
a2
Ob. 1 2
E. H.
Cl. 1 2
Bn. 1 2
Hn. 1 2
Hn. 3 4
Tpt. 1 2
Cor. 1 2
Trb. 1 2
3 Tuba
Timp.
S. D.
Cymb. B. D
Chimes
Perc.
Br. Band
Vn. 1
Vn. 2
Va.
Vc.
Cb.
fff

407
Picc.
Fl. 1 2
a2
Ob. 1 2
E. H.
Cl. 1 2
Bn. 1 2
Hn. 1 2 3 4
Tpt. 1 2
Cor. 1 2
Trb. 1 2 3
Tuba
Timp.
S. D.
Cymb. B. D
Perc.
Br. Band
407
Vn. 1 2
Va.
Vc.
Cb.

414
Picc.
fff
Fl. 1 2
Ob. 1 2
a2
E. H.
Cl. 1 2
Bn. 1 2
Hn. 1 2 3 4
Tpt. 1 2
a2
Cor. 1 2
a2
Trb. 1 2
a2
3 Tuba
Timp.
S. D.
Cymb. B. D
Perc.
Br. Band
414
Vn. 1 2
Va.
Vc.
Cb.
7

www.ingramcontent.com/pod-product-compliance
Lightning Source LLC
LaVergne TN
LVHW061340060426
835511LV00014B/2030